GREAT FISHING LIES of the WORLD

Tom Hepburn & Selwyn Jacobson

PRICE/STERN/SLOAN
Publishers, Inc., Los Angeles
1987

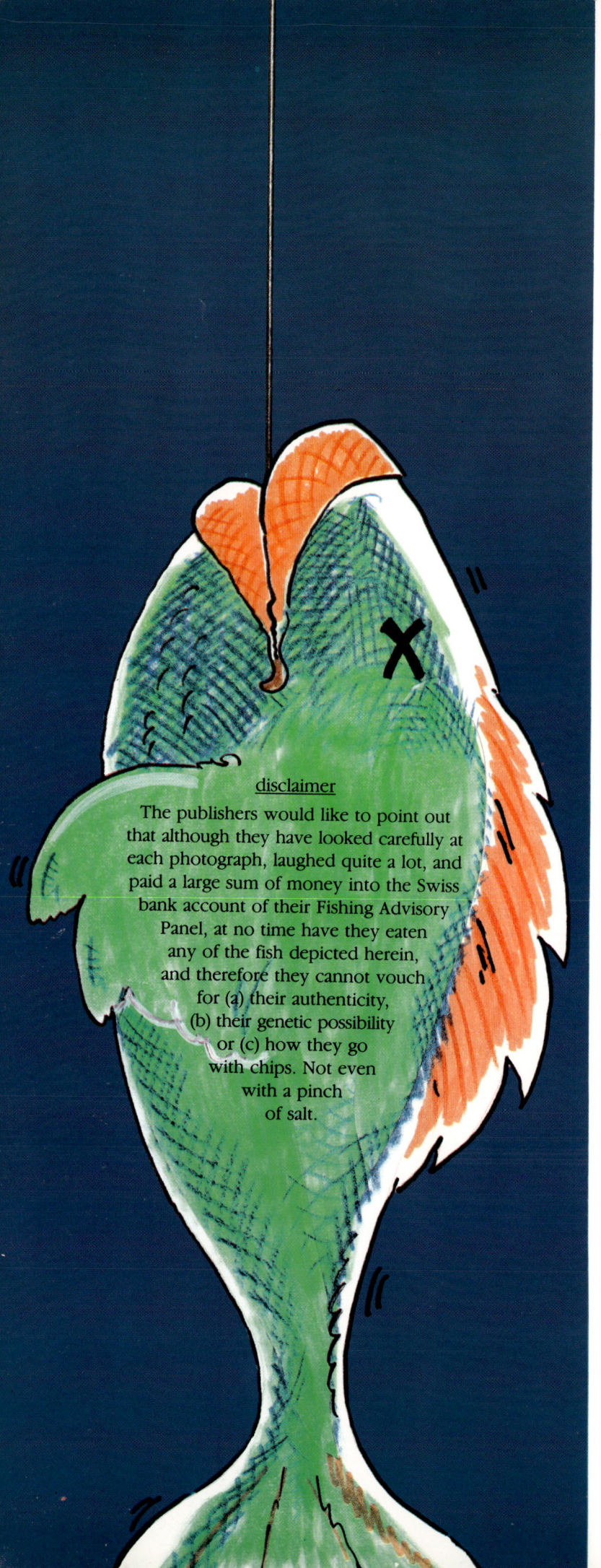

disclaimer
The publishers would like to point out that although they have looked carefully at each photograph, laughed quite a lot, and paid a large sum of money into the Swiss bank account of their Fishing Advisory Panel, at no time have they eaten any of the fish depicted herein, and therefore they cannot vouch for (a) their authenticity, (b) their genetic possibility or (c) how they go with chips. Not even with a pinch of salt.

Acknowledgements
Concept: Tom Hepburn & Selwyn Jacobson
Text: Tom Hepburn
Artwork: Grant Hanna
Illustrations: Rod Proud & Stu Duval
Design: Stu Duval & Selwyn Jacobson
Typesetting: Artspec Imaging Ltd
Printed in Hong Kong by Colorcraft

Copyright © 1986 by SeTo Publishing Ltd.
Published by Price/Stern/Sloan Publishers, Inc.
360 North La Cienega Boulevard, Los Angeles, California 90048

Printed in Hong Kong.

All rights reserved. No part of this publication may be reproduced, stored in a retrieval system or transmitted, in any form or by any means, electronic, mechanical, photocopying, recording or otherwise, without the prior written permission of the publisher.

ISBN 0-8431-1988-8

INTRODUCTION

Whether listening or telling, every fisherman loves a good tale — of the one that got away, and sometimes the one that didn't.

Of the most wonderful (but secret) hole in the world; of the strange things that happened when there was no one there to see (and verify?); of the ... well, the tales are legion, and a close look shows that they differ in just one respect.

Some are taller than others.

So, just to try and put these fishy stories in some kind of perspective, we have painstakingly gathered together a selection of the tallest ever told — and backed them up with photographs. And if *that* doesn't prove the point, I'll be a Dutch Canal trawlerman!

The purist among fishermen may wonder a little at our choice of locations. True, not everyone fishes regularly in Times Square, or in a seaquarium or even in an erupting geyser.

But who ever said fishermen were normal?

DOGGEREL BUNK

IT'S a tragic tale, but it should be told; to fish in unknown waters is bold but foolish, unless the arm is strong and the tackle new and the line is long.

So it happened one day, near the middle of December on a stretch of coast that could seldom boast a fish big enough to fill the dish of a hungry man. Remember?

Out in his boat (which could hardly float) with a lifelong friend there just to bend the convivial elbow, our hero struck luck (his bait was a duck!) and he hooked the fish you see.

The end of the story is not quite so nice; our man wrote a poem (it's been published twice). This posthumous verse could scarcely be worse, but it's repeated here as a warning most clear — if it's bigger than you, let it go!

"Oh I will go down to the sea again, to the lonely sea and the sky
And I will catch me a big one, and make my fisher-friends cry!
I'll pull it in with a wave and a grin and take it home for tea."
("I just never thought that the one I caught would be hungry enough to eat me!")

When a fish this size grabs the end of your line, it's almost immaterial what bait/tackle combination is being used. It is a matter of record though that the bait here was a worm on the end of a bent pin. Seems the angler had been studying the popular treatise on basic baits — "Long White Worms, and Where to Find Their Lairs," by B. Stoker.

BARCAROLE

THE Americans invented the floating crap game; New Zealanders have fun with their floating dollar; but only Aussies could come up with a floating Opera House!

No one on the Sydney Opera House Publicity Committee will admit to having thought up this unique way of pulling in a bit of off-season money, but it certainly is successful.

Releasing the series of titanium rods connected to the shore, and building a removable stern have enabled the structure to float. By judicious use of the roof, which acts as a series of fixed spinnakers, patrons can cruise in a leisurely fashion around the harbor, fishing while they listen to good music.

Ticket purchasers are presented with a free bucket of garlic prawns, either for use as bait or to nibble during the entr'acte.

Locals believe this lethal combination can catch a fish as quickly as it can end a beautiful friendship; a good technique is required in either case.

HOLEY MACKEREL

NEW YORK attracts many people for many reasons, so it is perhaps not too surprising that the recent series of viciously cold, hard winters has provided its own special attraction for out-of-towners.

Like most of his people from the far north, who have proved they can adjust to a severe climate better than any other group in the world, Karluk is a nomad who ranges far and wide in a continuous search for food.

Hearing during a Caribou hunt of a mysterious "Frozen Apple", he traveled south for the winter and (like many an ethnic minority) made his home in Times Square.

Here, comfortably if simply housed, he utilizes his traditional fishing skills to provide for himself, his wife (well, *somebody's* wife) and his children.

Eskimos often use an ice-fishing jig through a circular hole cut in the ice. And with the Arctic ice sheet up to 14,000′ thick in places, it is important to know where to cut! In more temperate climes, though, a manhole cover will do quite well, and a line dropped down, no matter how it is baited, usually brings results. Anything, in fact, from a dead City employee to a live alligator.

Karluk prefers his own Jig design, finding the local fish strangely attracted to his modified Chrysler hubcap. The hook comes from an abandoned towtruck.
Note the Baby Alligator Trap and the Foul Objects Probe — both essential for selective fishing.

YUM KIPPER

CANADIAN salmon are second only to their Scottish cousins when it comes to flavor (New Zealand, Argentinian and Rumanian fall way behind), but in some instances it can be argued that they prove more fun to catch.

This well-known salmon leap, not far from the Canadian/U.S. border, offers an unusual test of angling skill, and is the more interesting in that, for a mere $5.00, any tourist can hire rod, tackle, raincoat, and sou'wester and be "licensed" for 15 minutes, during which he may land and keep as many fish as the Fates decree.

Because of the small fishing area, it *can* become confusing; for example, when several buses unload their tourist hordes at the same time. Lines can become crossed, and arguments about who caught which fish have been known to lead to fisticuffs. Normally, however, the innate good temper and basic decency of your average fisherman tend to keep the peace.

Local conditions have brought about an intriguing variation on the salmon spinning rod, with an improved bait-throwing capacity of up to 6lbs.

For an extra $2.50 rods come equipped with the motorized "Devon Kipper" (J.B. McBaffie, pat. pending), a fly which has a fatal attraction for Scotch salmon — though, oddly, not for Jewfish — and is growing in popularity here. An unusual feature of this lure its its ability to swim up waterfalls in pursuit of prey.

WHALE OF A TAIL

SOMETIMES, when a discreet Mrs. Simpson flicked across a silent pool fails to excite, when a line hurled 100 yards over a raging surf decries delicacy, when a stick of gelignite dropped at dead of night into a salmon river seems to lack finesse, then the dedicated fisherman knows he must seek a greater challenge!

In Miami a group of confirmed anglers believe they have found just that. Each year they get together at the Seaquarium for their annual Fisherman Of The Year Contest. The Killer Whale tank is stocked with yellowtail shipped in especially for the occasion, and contestants descend in pairs into the tank to begin battle. Trained attendants — one to each angler — are obligatory since the unfortunate day in '79 when Firestone J. Bardahl disappeared from view, never to be seen again. (His surf-rod now hangs in memoriam above the mantel in the Members' Bar.) These attendants distract the Killer Whales while contestants fish — first man to land his trout goes on to the next round. Club officials are pleased to point out that they haven't lost an attendant yet.

A surf rod, using fixed ball reels, is recommended.
Most popular bait is a small lamb chop. Spare chops slung in a bag round the neck can, in moments of stress, be tossed to circling Killer Whales.

page 14

COD WAR & PLACE

DURING the heady days of the Great British Cod War (now, alas, naught but a gleam in a butcher's eye) only friends and relatives first feared, then mourned for the crew of the *Resolution II*.

Sent out on a night attack into the Icelandic 200-mile zone, the vessel mysteriously disappeared, and was never seen or heard from again . . . until reports began filtering through of a strange and ghostly trawler appearing and disappearing seemingly at will within the complicated canal complex in Holland!

The media of course wrote knowingly of the *Marie Celeste* and the *Mary Deare*, hinting that ghost ships sail in threes — but nothing could be confirmed until this remarkable photograph was taken (by a drunken Irish tourist on a "Common Market in Four Days" bus tour).

Students of the occult will immediately note two things: the trawler is *clearly invisible* to the couple sitting on the skiff by the bank, and the fishermen are *successfully catching cod!* There are obvious questions.

Can the ghost trawler be seen only by intoxicated Irishmen? Is the couple on the skiff blinded by love? What is the significance of *three* windmills? (One for each ghost ship?) Are the cod (a) edible and (b) less than $5.00 per lb? Alas, these and other pointless questions will probably not be answered until the trawler comes out of its time warp and reappears in the North Sea.

CLAWS SHAVE

THOSE who choose to fish in man-made impounds may be looked at askance by those of their brethren who prefer the rugged splendor of a high-country river, but it can be argued that, as a regular source of food, impounds are hard to beat.

Here in the Western Australia desert the creation of such impounds brought at once a blessing and a curse. The local Pinna Cales tribe, long accustomed to a rigid diet of Kangaroo cutlets and Dingo stew, was delighted to add fresh fish to its menu. Alas, so attached did the tribe become to the delectable Murray River Cod that midnight poaching excursions became the rule rather than the exception, and now this fish is believed to be no more!

Yabbies* remain the ideal live bait here, but a new strain of Sand Crab, developed at the nearby Dr. Moreau Institute for Improving on Nature is becoming popular.

The crabs are trained to tug on the line with their short claw after grasping a fish with the longer appendage, thus doing away with the need for hooks, sinkers, floats — and in some instances, fingers.

*fresh water cray

OH, BLOW

DEVELOPED from the near-defunct pastime of Codwalloping, Fish Hammering is the latest craze to sweep the seabeds of the world.

Strict rules govern this puerile and useless activity; length, weight, shape and striking area of hammers are rigorously controlled by the Min. of Ag. & Fish., whose inspectors patrol random coastlines in a continuous search (often in unmarked diving suits) for illegal hammerers.

In some countries — eg., Australia and New Zealand — Hammering Blitzes are now legal, and an unsuspecting hammerer, just out for a few casual blows with his pals, can find himself dredged to one side, and, before he knows what's happening, have his implement measured by an official ruler! Instant loss of license follows if guilt is proved — witness poor Aaron Groat, who had cleverly designed his striking surface in the shape of a fish.

He may have lost his license, but he does have the satisfaction of having owned the first Sharkheaded Hammer.

page 20

STONED FISH

A FEW years back, geologically speaking, the British coastline went in and out in different places than it does today. Ben Nevis was but an atoll, East Anglia hadn't even surfaced, and an Ichthyosaur was spotted by a Pict as far up the Thames as Henley.

Around 3000 years ago, when France was still far enough away not to give Brits offense, Salisbury Bay was a pretty seaside resort popular with holidaymakers of every tribe. On its calm, almost tideless waters, boating and fishing, fairly new sports, were indulged in by the moneyed Druid class. It was this group of trendsetters who developed the now forgotten fishing technique of pouring large quantities of Mead into shallow pools and hurling rocks at the fish who came gasping to the surface.

The stone structure seen in our photograph is believed to be the first Coracle Marina in Ancient Britain.

Cunningly carved into the shape of a (prehistoric) stonefly — stonemasons were devilish cunning around 1800 B.C. — this lure was very popular with Druids for catching stonefish, even though these were (a) venomous and (b) found only in the tropics. It just goes to show you: Druids weren't <u>that</u> smart

WHITEWASH

IN a continuing search to include new thrills to the sedentary sport of trout fishing, a small group of intrepid anglers has added a dash of spice to a day on the river.

By indulging in a bit of whitewater rafting, they have given new meaning to the terms casting, stalking and laminar flow.

The problem is, though, that some pretty strange fish find their way up into these turbulent torrents, and it is best to come well prepared for any eventuality. Make sure your flies are properly tied before leaving shore, that your spare harpoons have little rubber tips on the end, and that you keep a spray can of shark repellent in your lunchbox.

Speed of strike is of the essence if you want your trout or salmon for dinner. The newly developed Blunderpoon gun reduces the chance factor.

BARELY POSSIBLE

Brown Bear: *"Haven't had a bite for ages!"*

Polar Bear: *"must be your bait — I caught one <u>this</u> size only yesterday."*

WHICH just goes to prove that when it comes to landing trout, technique and equipment are important, but being at the right spot at the right time is essential.

(Note: Students of animal migratory patterns who are perhaps puzzled to see a Polar and a Brown Bear in seemingly friendly coexistence should not worry unduly — there is an explanation. The Brown Bear was born in Alberta and lives nearby; the Polar fellow worked his way up country from a wayward iceberg, and plans on returning to the Arctic for Summer.)

Bare bait seems appropriate, if a bit self-defeating; but even fishermen (?) get peckish sometimes. Maybe the key to good fishing here is the skeleton variety?

AQU-AYRE-IUM

WHEN the Australian Northern Territories C.D.&T. Board*
decided to spend the money left for its exclusive use by deceased Dingo fancier
Chauncey Lupe on a combined emergency water/fishing pool, few locals thought much
of the idea.

But succeed it did, to the point where tourists flock from all over the free fishing
world, just to say they've caught a trout on Ayers Rock.

Thanks partly to the input of the late Lupe, the fish have been bred to rise only for
dehydrated Dingo — surely some sort of rough poetic justice?

*Catchment, Dingo & Tourist

The unusual qualities of desiccated Dingo are
strangely efficacious in this area. There's something
about this much-maligned mammal that makes fish
(like the Australian Press) rise to the bait whenever
its name is mentioned around the Rock.

HALF-BAKED HAUL

ROTORUA in New Zealand is known the world over for both its incredible thermal activity and its fabulous trout and game fishing.

Now, thanks to a recently discovered series of linked underground tunnels leading from the thermal and volcanic center some 30 miles to the Eastern seaboard, a new type of fishing is becoming popular.

Within this subterranean maze, where the temperature remains a steady 115°C the fish breed and develop in a partially cooked state. And when caught in a geyser eruption (as in our photograph), they can, if played carefully, be landed ready to eat. Access to these pools is therefore strictly limited, and a recently approved Government regulation has added the name of the *ROTORUA MUDLIN* to those of the Marlin and the Shark on the list of specified trophy fish.

Lord Atten of Burgh, prominent zoologist and TV front man, has examined this unique hard-fighting fish and believes it is a distant relative of the mudfish of the Indian continent. As a newly discovered subspecies, it has been officially named Thermus wotawopawopa from Whakarewarewa!

A fly which has proved useful in taking this fish is the *MUDDLER MINNOW*. Because of the asbestos fibre required in its construction it is recommended that a face mask be worn when tying. Such high-tech bait needs, of course, a modified surf casting rod.

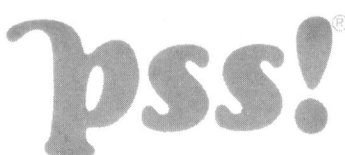

PRICE/STERN/SLOAN *Publishers, Inc.*
360 North La Cienega Boulevard, Los Angeles, California 90048